# New-Model Scholarship: How Will It Survive?

by Abby Smith

March 2003

Council on Library and Information Resources

Washington, D.C.

## About the Author

Abby Smith is director of programs at CLIR. She is responsible for developing and managing collaboration with key library and archival institutions to ensure long-term access to our cultural and scholarly heritage. Before joining CLIR in 1997, she had worked at the Library of Congress for nine years, first as a consultant to the special collections divisions, then as coordinator of several cultural and academic programs in the offices of the Librarian of Congress and the Associate Librarian for Library Services. She is the author of *Why Digitize?* and *Strategies for Building Digitized Collections*, and coauthor of *Managing Cultural Assets from a Business Perspective*, and *The Evidence at Hand: Report of the Task Force on the Artifact in Library Collections*.

ISBN 1-887334-99-8

Published by:

**Council on Library and Information Resources**
**1755 Massachusetts Avenue, NW, Suite 500**
**Washington, DC 20036**
Web site at http://www.clir.org

Additional copies are available for $15 per copy. Orders must be placed through CLIR's Web site.

 The paper in this publication meets the minimum requirements of the American National Standard for Information Sciences—Permanence of Paper for Printed Library Materials ANSI Z39.48-1984.

# Contents

## Preface

In 2002, the Alfred P. Sloan Foundation, which for several years has been supporting Web-based projects to document the history of contemporary science and technology, turned to the library and archival community for guidance on how the foundation's data creators could preserve their digital documents. With a generous grant to the Council on Library and Information Resources (CLIR), the foundation sought to engage those who are best positioned to advise on digital preservation issues.

CLIR hosted a meeting of scholars, librarians, archivists, technologists, publishers, and funders to discuss the preservation of digital scholarly resources. The goal of the workshop was to identify the needs of various stakeholders—Web site creators; distributors and publishers of digital materials; representatives of archives, libraries, and repositories that want to collect these sites and make them available; end users; and anyone in the chain of scholarly communication who might want to discover and use these works for their own purposes—and to agree on common approaches to meeting those needs.

The needs, it turns out, are great, and the approaches not yet clear. Discussions of preservation needs included those of large-scale databases in the sciences and the published electronic record in all disciplines, but the participants' central concern was the complex needs of the digital resources documenting contemporary actions and ideas—digital objects that are created outside the library and seldom developed expressly for publication. These are wholly new types of information resources, so novel that no common term except "digital objects" or "sites" can describe them. To get a sense of what is under construction and how complicated these sites tend to be, data creators from the Dibner Institute at the Massachusetts Institute of Technology, George Mason University, and the University of Virginia presented their Web-based work, spoke about what they were trying to achieve, and defined what they perceived as barriers to creation and longevity. Librarians, archivists, publishers, and others discussed how they are grappling with the problems presented by the complex and often unstructured digital objects that arrive on their doorsteps, too often unannounced, to be preserved. All participants tried to identify the work to be done to ensure digital object longevity and to articulate the new roles and responsibilities that all stakeholders in the research community must embrace to be good stewards of scholarly resources.

This report is informed by the lively discussions that took place at that conference, and by two papers that were circulated in advance and which are included as Appendixes 1 and 2. Although based on much of the information shared and knowledge created at that meeting, the report takes those conversations as a point of departure only. It does not attempt to report in detail on the meeting itself or on the views of its participants. Rather, this document attempts to describe the scope of problems posed by preserving Web-based scholarly resources. It focuses on "new-model scholarship"—scholarship that is born digital and constitutes an important source for present and future research and teaching. The new-model scholarship is, specifically, the variety of Web sites and other desktop digital objects that faculty and graduate students are creating that fall somewhere short of "published" but are worthy of access into the future. A strict distinction between primary and secondary sources is neither possible nor desirable in the digital objects under discussion, as the report shows. The report is not intended to be comprehensive in its review of current activities. Furthermore, the projects and preservation initiatives mentioned do not pretend to be typical, but are rather exemplary of the range of aspirations held and actions undertaken by leading innovators in digital content creation.

In "Moving Forward," several ideas are advanced for short- and long-term steps to address the growing problem of digital stewardship. These are modest proposals suggesting promising directions that can realistically be taken. Special attention is paid to identifying all the sectors in higher education that will be responsible for ensuring the future of scholarship and its resources. Much progress was made in 2002. Digital preservation has become a vital concern to many outside libraries and archives. The federal government, chiefly through programs of the National Archives and the Library of Congress, has challenged the library, archival, and research and development communities to address what it perceives to be a serious civic problem sooner rather than later. Our hope is to engage those who see preservation as a crucial element in the stewardship of scholarly resources and to point to ways in which each member of the research community can contribute to the public good that such stewardship serves.

CLIR is grateful to the Sloan Foundation for its support and to the many leaders in digital librarianship, scholarship, and publishing who contributed their time and energy to explore a difficult and urgent problem.

# NEW-MODEL SCHOLARSHIP: HEADED FOR EARLY OBSOLESENCE?

The Internet has transformed the way in which scholarship is produced and disseminated, most notably in the sciences. In the humanities and social sciences, digital technologies for scholarly research, analysis, communication, and teaching have been adopted more slowly, but there has been significant innovation even in these fields. There has been enough progress that libraries and special collecting institutions are concerned about how to acquire, preserve, and make accessible some of the digital content coming from historians, literary scholars, and other humanists, as well as the primary sources in digital format on which this scholarship is based.

Most scholars who are creating digital information are seeking ways to make the best use of the technologies at hand to further research, discovery, and the sharing of results. In the scientific community, where currency of information is at a premium, this has led to such innovations as the establishment of preprint archives in high-energy physics and mathematics that are managed by the data creators. Certain fields, such as genomics, are building massive databases that require the attention of information management specialists in an academic domain—bioinformatics in this case. Scientific communities of knowledge develop and manage their own information nodes on the Web to speed communication in time and across space. They can thus create a community of scientists around the globe who have access to essentially the same information with few of the sociological or physical barriers that previously existed. Such sites as the preprint archive for high-energy physics (arXiv.org) are not intended to stand in for or replace peer-reviewed publication, nor are they intended to be "archival" in the sense that the fields creating them view them as "of record" and necessarily persistent. The sites are something new: technology allows an old need—timely communication—to be met in innovative ways, yielding a new model of scholarly output.

The humanities, which work with much less money and on a smaller scale than "big science," have not seen similar growth in building common information resources and managing them collectively. Innovators in the use of digital technology in the humanities often work singly or in small teams; creators of information must address major data management problems on their own or turn, belatedly, to their campus library to help them preserve and manage their handcrafted sites and databases. This is a cause of increasing concern to digital librarians, who confront in this growing phenomenon a series of preservation challenges different from those they have seen until now with electronic journals. Although scholarly electronic journals present many intellectual property issues besides format and version challenges, they present few problems in selection or assessment for enduring value. E-journals are in the mainstream of genres that form the core of academic collection development. Their value is known, and they do not come as "one-offs" in nonstandard formats.

What will happen to these new models of scholarship? Although it is impossible to predict how such scholarship will develop, it is not too early to focus on the question of their long-term value and longevity. How will they be assessed for enduring value, and how long will they survive?

These are basic questions that preservationists in all media face daily. Preservation is that series of actions that individuals and institutions take to ensure that a given resource will be accessible for use at some unknown time. To preserve effectively, one must be able to anticipate what those future uses might be and then develop policies and procedures to safeguard the information.

New-model scholarship poses novel challenges to preservationists: How do we know what the value of these digital objects is and may be decades hence? How do we anticipate and address the technical needs of fragile digital objects over time? Who is responsible for preservation, and how is it financed? Librarians and archivists have been working on these issues for more than a decade, but they will not be able to answer these questions alone.

Preservation has been a back-room library operation for many years. Patrons are seldom aware of this work unless a resource is lost or too damaged to provide useful information. In the analog realm, most scholars understand that preservation goes well beyond "passive restraints" on aging and damage, but they rarely give the matter much attention. The burden of collecting and preserving materials for future access does not normally impinge directly on the scholar or creator, especially for published materials. It is the responsibility of publishers and libraries. As for unpublished materials—such as the manuscripts, maps, photographs, and audio tapes found in archives and special collections in research libraries—few scholars are responsible for building primary source collections from scratch or curating them, let alone taking measures to help ensure their long-term survival. Most researchers rely on archivists and librarians to collect, preserve, and make accessible the key resources on which discovery and scholarship are based. A major exception to this rule is found in such fields as ethnomusicology and anthropology, which are based on observational data.

In the digital realm, by contrast, the critical dependency of preservation on good stewardship begins with the act of creation, and the creator has a decisive role in the longevity of the digital object. This is a new role for most scholars—one for which their professional training has seldom prepared them. The role is fraught with unhappy implications for the use of the scholars' time, daunting demands to acquire new skills, and the uncertainties that come with dependencies on hardware and software, and also on librarians and archivists, to cope with the complicated tasks of data management.

For the digital scholar intent on creating information resources that are long-lived and can be accessed easily, the task is not only to invent tools that foster productive use of the Web as a medium of scholarship and teaching but also to create material in preservable form.

In the past decade, digital librarians and archivists have worked hard to define the parameters of "material in preservable form." They have tried to specify which formats and encoding schemes will hold up the best through one or more cycles of data migration. Because of their often-prescriptive nature, these efforts have met with mixed success in the academic community.

## New-Model Scholarship: Three Examples

Developing strategies for preserving digital resources of high research value should begin with a look at the aspirations of digital scholars. An understanding of what these scholars are trying to achieve and an examination of the challenges they face should inform approaches to ensure the longevity of digital objects. The examples that follow describe three scholarly projects that share crucial dependencies on Web-based technologies and illustrate many problems creators face today. The examples cover a wide range of fields in the humanities—the history of current science and technology, history, and literary studies—yet they have several common aspirations, approaches, and challenges.

### History of Recent Science and Technology, the Dibner Institute (hrst.mit.edu)[1]

The History of Recent Science and Technology (HRST), funded by the Alfred P. Sloan Foundation and located at the Dibner Institute at the Massachusetts Institute of Technology (MIT), is attempting to document specific fields in contemporary science and engineering. Scholars at the Dibner Institute believe that the history of science must keep pace with science itself, and that it is not well served by the practice of one scholar focusing on one scientist and writing a biographical study. Science comprises massive projects that involve large collaborations of scientists and technicians who work in highly specialized fields of inquiry. HRST is developing a historical methodology that it believes is well suited to documenting this phenom-

---

[1] The author thanks Babak Ashrafi of the Dibner Institute for providing information and advice about this project.

enon as well as the results of the scientific research itself. They have created groups of historians who collaborate on documenting these large projects through Web-based networks. They are recruiting support from technologists, librarians and archivists, and the historical actors—the scientists and engineers themselves.

One of five projects on the site, the Physics of Scales has three historians who make up the core team of principal investigators. They are recruiting about two dozen scientists who have worked in the physics of scales. The core team will interview the scientists, put their working papers and documents online, and collaborate with them to annotate the documents. They will then ask a few of these scientists to moderate forums that will yield yet more primary source documentation. These scientists, in other words, will become "communication nodes" who will recruit other collaborators and students to contribute their own documentation to the site. By the end of the project, HRST hopes to have online interviews with 60 to 80 scientists that document aspects of the field they pioneered. In effect, the core team is trying to develop networks that then create their own networks, each in turn creating a documentary trail. Given the inherent difficulties in motivating the subjects of a historical study—in this case, scientists and engineers—to take hours of their time to document their past and present activities, the Physics of Scales core team has tried to develop a process that minimizes the technical and procedural barriers to participation. This has not been easy.

A major technical problem has been the need for a trade-off between standardizing formats, which is good for digital preservation, and allowing data entry to be customized, which the historians creating the site perceive as essential to their work. Although the historians have encouraged the scientists to use certain XML standards to enable important digital library features, their efforts have not always been successful. The historians realize they must make it as simple as possible for scientists to contribute to the body of knowledge. Therefore, they decided not to impose any required standards. The historians also gave top priority to creating tools that can be easily customized by the core team. They did this to put the historians who serve as site moderators firmly in charge of structuring the online interactions among the scientist participants. They hoped thereby to ensure that the contents would be historically significant and worthy of preserving.[2]

Early in the project, the HRST historians decided to use an open source toolkit that allows them to annotate documents, create extensible time lines, produce highly detailed bibliographies, conduct interviews, and enable scores of scientists and engineers to discuss

---

[2] From the archival viewpoint, the documents created in the course of this project are not records, that is, texts and other forms of recorded information that are generated in the course of doing business. This might raise some concerns about the value of these sources over time, concerns well understood by, for example, scholars who gather documentary evidence from firsthand accounts. It also means that, because the self-documenting by scientists does not occur in the course of normal business, the documents created will be less comprehensive than records.

their fields. They favored these tools because using them does not require much technical knowledge. This approach contrasts with that of the Perseus project (www.perseus.tufts.edu), where the scholars are the programmers: when they need a tool, they know how to write it. The Physics of Scales project hired a programmer and a graphic designer. HRST also had to decide between ease of use (text only) and the physical attractiveness of the site (buttons rather than text links). They chose ease of use.

The project is now in its third year. The software that has enabled data gathering is finished, but the digital library software that will allow users to extract the richness of information is not. That digital library work has taken a backseat to creating the scholarly documents. Preservation planning has also been put off, and the core team is only now beginning to discuss how it will secure a library's commitment to acquire and sustain the output of the project. Although not ideal, this process is typical and in some ways hard to avoid. The creators were fully occupied with the short-term goal of creating something of value from a historian's point of view. They had little time to plan simultaneously for preserving something that was being created in an iterative fashion.

The Physics of Scales project exemplifies many key features of new-model scholarly enterprises. It is

- experimental: designed to develop and model a methodology for generating recorded information about a scientific enterprise that might otherwise go undocumented.
- open-ended: generates digital objects that are intended to be added to over time.
- interactive: gathers content through dynamic interactions among the participants. The historians stipulate that the interactions, as well as the content, are part of what is to be preserved.
- software-intensive: stipulates that the tools for using the data are as valuable a part of the project as is the content, and thus worthy of equal attention by preservationists.
- multimedia: creates information in a variety of genres—texts, time lines, images—and of file formats.
- unpublished: designed to be used and disseminated through the Web, yet not destined to be published formally or submitted for peer review.

### Center for History and New Media, George Mason University (chnm.gmu.edu)[3]

Some members of the history faculty at George Mason University (GMU) have created the Center for History and New Media to explore new ways of creating historical documents. Like the historians in the HRST, these scholars do not wish to become experts in technology. They see technology as a tool that can enable them to expand the historical resource base and its functionality. The promise

[3] The author thanks Roy Rosenzweig of George Mason University for information and advice about the Center for History and New Media projects.

of this technology is, as one historian explains, to open the writing of history to a host of new voices and new stories, to create a more democratic and inclusive view of the past, to offer modes of learning about the past that spur student participation and engagement, and to engender innovative scholarship that challenges traditional ways of "doing history."

The site creators have placed a high value on experimentation and sharing knowledge, and have consciously tolerated "make-do" use of the technology. The formats they have created so far include text, image, audio, video, e-mail, database, hypertext, and interactive programs. Although proud of its accomplishments, the Center acknowledges having slighted standards and preservation as it focused on the short term more than on the long term. This approach is typical of that of other startup enterprises. Moreover, it is unlikely that they would have been able to accomplish as much as they have if they had focused on the long term. Now, however, they are at the point where they must begin to extend their focus into the future.

The twin demands of scholarship and preservation create tension. The site creators were able to avoid this tension in their early projects by declaring their activities "experimental." For example, in 1999 GMU undertook a project with *The American Quarterly*, the flagship journal in American studies, to present hypertext scholarship. The goal was to move beyond hypertext theory and create examples. The project team chose not to work with Project Muse at Johns Hopkins University (JHU), which publishes the online version of *The American Quarterly*, so that it could obviate the problems that might arise when creating a product that departed from JHU's standardized format. Creating an experimental, nonstandard project was one of GMU's objectives.

For other projects, the team has thought more about the longevity of its digital objects, because their goal is to create enduring historical resources. Their current projects are not designed to be experimental, although they do suffer from tensions between the need to achieve some short-term goals and to create with longevity in mind. For example, the 9/11 Project, designed to gather testimonies from people around the country about their experiences on September 11, 2001, was inaugurated under great time pressure. The team had only one month to launch the site, and it was impossible to foresee and act on the variety of preservation issues that might arise. The historians already see problems that may in the end compromise the value of the sources that they have created. These potential problems originate from the need to act expediently: they were not able to create the deep metadata that will provide future evidence of the records' authenticity.

Like the historians of the Physics of Scales project, the GMU team finds it necessary to lower technical barriers and reduce time commitments of the volunteer participants to ensure a critical mass of contributions. While collecting stories to document the effects of 9/11 on individuals, for example, the GMU team decided to demand only "barebones data" from and about the contributors. They felt that if they were to require more, then contributions would drop off significantly. The team had assessed the National Endowment for the Humanities (NEH) project, "My History Is America's History," which collected more metadata than GMU's 9/11 project did and thus promised a possibly richer site in the end. But the team concluded that, because it takes a significant effort to fill out the NEH forms, NEH was able to collect only as many stories in two and a half years as GMU collected in two and a half months, despite the publicity afforded the NEH project by a cover story in *Parade* magazine.

GMU's 9/11 site continues to grow; about 15,000 stories are available. Discussions are under way with a national institution to preserve the 9/11 site. Faculty members are also discussing with GMU ways to ensure persistence for other Center projects. Interestingly, the NEH site, which chose depth of contribution at the expense of breadth of coverage, has been discontinued and is no longer accessible on the Web.

Like the HRST sites, GMU sites are experimental, open-ended, and interactive. They represent a complex mix of formats and genres. They are clearly created for wide dissemination, even though they fall outside the well-known publishing norms. The libraries with which the Center is negotiating for long-term deposit understand the value of a site such as 9/11, in that it documents a major event in the history of the United States. It is also valuable as evidence of a new and rapidly evolving information technology. Such sites are, in effect, "digital incunables," and may be as prized over time as fifteenth-century imprints are today. Historians at the Center advocate for a digital preservation strategy that, like GMU's projects, favors action over deliberation and has built-in assessments and course corrections that are familiar in computer science, where an iterative process of "learn as you go" can result in significant advances.

### Institute for Advanced Technology in the Humanities, University of Virginia (www.iath.virginia.edu)[4]

A third set of examples of new-model scholarship comes from the Institute for Advanced Technology in the Humanities (IATH) at the University of Virginia (UVA), which has supported humanities projects that use technology as a research tool for close to a decade. IATH has several projects that are built of complex, heterogeneous file format types. They are still growing and showcase the challenges of incorporating successive generations of content, contributors, and software.

*The William Blake Archive*, for example, which brings together into one virtual space a variety of source materials by and about Blake from many institutions, is among the oldest of the IATH sites. Over the years, differences of opinion have risen about what good digital library standards allow creators to do and what creators want

---

4 The author thanks John Unsworth, of the University of Virginia's Institute for Advanced Technologies in the Humanities, for information and advice on IATH projects.

to do. For example, staff members of the Blake Archive are intensely concerned with reproducing the quality of physical artifacts and the site is designed to allow a user to examine closely a surrogate image of a plate on which William Blake engraved illustrated poems. IATH established an approach to structuring the data that appropriately privileges the physical structure of a volume over its logical structure. When the scholars later decided the table of contents ought to list the poems, not merely the plates, IATH had to create ways to cut across the privilege hierarchy.

*Monuments and Dust*, a site devoted to the culture of Victorian London, renders its content dynamically, presenting a challenge to creator and preserver alike. It includes a three-dimensional model of the Crystal Palace showing every nut, bolt, wire, and pane of glass in the original. Created in an architectural modeling program (Form•Z), rendered in a lighting simulation program (Radiance), animated, and delivered in Quick Time, the site is very difficult to standardize into a digital library format because few standards of the XML/SGML type exist for such models. The demand for these types of complex and dynamic format types is common among architects and landscape architects, for example, with whom IATH does much of its work. Until the digital preservation community develops and promotes preservation standards in areas such as these, *Monuments and Dust* and similar projects are fated to be ephemeral.

The Rossetti Archive (properly titled *The Complete Writings and Pictures of Dante Gabriel Rossetti: A Hypermedia Research Archive*) is another early project of IATH. It originated as text (SGML, then XML) and images. Much of the scholarly work is found in the illustration. The archive now contains about 10,000 files and 45,000 cross-references in various languages, and it continues to grow. The references include songs and digitized films, among other complex formats. The second of four planned installments of new materials was mounted in the summer of 2002. It defines itself as a hypertextual instrument designed to facilitate scholarly research, not as content per se. The content, both reformatted and wholly original, is one part of the larger whole. Therefore, ensuring future access to the Rossetti Archive does not mean just securing the preservation of the content.

## What Do These Examples Tell Us?

The three projects just described illustrate several challenges to preservation that are typical of work in the humanities. First, the digital objects created are often complex, composed of heterogeneous types, open ended, and resistant to closure and to normalization. Moreover, the functionalities that scholars prize may often be at odds with emerging best practices for preservation as well as with one another.

Of the three endeavors, IATH is the oldest and best positioned to address some of these challenges. Indeed, because of IATH's commitment to pioneering technology in the humanities, it has partnered with the University of Virginia Libraries' Digital Library Research and Development Group in a project to address three related problems:

- scholarly use of digital primary resources
- library adoption of born-digital scholarly research
- co-creation of digital resources by scholars, publishers, and libraries

The project, titled "Supporting Digital Scholarship" and funded by The Andrew W. Mellon Foundation, is designed to identify problems associated with preserving materials that originate outside libraries. Much of the material created in this fashion may be sponsored by a research institute and be designed for publication, but if it is to endure, it will need to be supported by a repository that will ensure its integrity, authenticity, and accessibility into the future. Traditionally, that repository has been a library. Will it be a library in the future, or are other possibilities evolving?

IATH is trying to articulate new roles for all the institutions and individuals that have traditionally played well-defined roles in the production, dissemination, and long-term care of scholarly resources. They are especially concerned that neither libraries nor publishers are able to deal with the digital objects coming from the sorts of collaborations they foster. Understanding the distinction that some digital librarians make between the "presentation form" and the "archival form" of a digital object, and the work entailed in transforming the former into the latter, some at IATH suggest that the publisher's role is to take material originating in digital form and produce it in a format that libraries can collect for long-term retention as well as contemporary access (i.e., with standardized metadata and sustainable formats). They point out that in the print regime, the publisher is responsible for editing, printing, binding, and delivering a text to a library and argue that in the digital realm, these activities should take place at an equally high institutional level. Responsibility for these activities should not be based on a negotiation between the digital author and the librarian, as is often the case today.

Normalizing a digital object for preservation is one area under negotiation between author and archive. Librarians would like to see creators adhere to standard, preservation-friendly formats. Authors do not like to be inhibited by such parameters, and they also do not like to create the amount of metadata usually required for preservation. Ironically, in the IATH projects, insufficient documentation of the digital object is seldom the problem in normalizing it for preservation; extensive documentation exists for all of IATH's projects. Rather, sites produced by scholars tend to overload some file names with too much information, resulting in ambiguities that cause problems even for the originator. Publishers have knowledge that can be applied to developing and maintaining digital materials and to recovering ongoing production costs. Even a well-tagged, well-described object may lose its identity over time and become irretrievable, unless a "persistent identifier" had been assigned to it. In the view of some at IATH, publishers are ideally positioned to mitigate this problem as well.

## Who Should be Responsible for Safekeeping?

The suggestion that publishers assume certain critical functions of "digital librarianship" raises its own concerns. For some, the idea that digital preservation, or at least some of its key functions, would become the responsibility of commercial or nonprofit entities that come and go in the marketplace is unacceptable. Preservation, they argue, should be the responsibility of institutions that are buffered from the vicissitudes of business cycles. But do such institutions exist? Libraries are not entirely unaffected by upswings and downturns in the economy. They are not currently prepared to recover the added expenses of the preservation services that digital media demand. Many analog collections are "preserved" in libraries and archives through simple accessioning and storing, and no other investments are made to prolong the useful life of the resource. Libraries are underfunded for the tasks of analog preservation. They cannot assume sole responsibility for the added burdens of digital preservation.

The debate will continue about whether publishers will be ready, willing, and able to provide the types of preservation services just mentioned, but in truth, the discussion may not be relevant to the new-model scholarly resources that HRST and GMU are creating. These sites, after all, are not destined for publication as their primary form of dissemination. HRST sites are, at present, designed for archival deposit, that is, to serve as primary source materials for the secondary literature that publishers see. Repurposing may be desirable at some point, either for publishing or for use in teaching, but the HRST data creators have not provided for that. Their sites are collections of archival materials that, in the analog realm, would go to a special collections library without being published.

## How Do We Decide What to Preserve?

For many scholarly sites, such as those mounted by the Center for History and New Media, there is no clear-cut audience to help acquisitions librarians determine the suitability of the sites for library users. The sites at GMU have a variety of uses: some are meant for teaching purposes, some as primary source material, some for the general public; still others have mixed target audiences. Part of the reason for getting as much material online as quickly as possible has been to see who is attracted to the sites and how users interact with them. There is always a greater use of a "scholarly" site by the public than is anticipated. Although the nature of that use can be difficult to assess, it is nonetheless something that historians such as those at GMU want to consider and, if possible, encourage.

Another challenge for acquisitions lies in that these sites collectively do not pass through the quality filters provided by publication. This raises the types of technical issues for digital material seen in the IATH projects described above. Perhaps most significant, lack of peer review or the vetting that customarily underlies decisions about publishing makes selection more difficult for librarians. Also, publication information (who published, when, and in what number) has always been critical in helping librarians evaluate items under consideration for acquisition.

Another feature of new-model scholarship presenting novel choices for librarians is that these sites do not always contain new content and that the content of the site itself is not always the chief offering to the scholar and teacher. The Physics of Scales site has created a resource that gathers important and unique information, but does so in conjunction with specific functionalities that are crucial to using the data. Those functionalities are similar to the instrumentation found in laboratories—instrumentation that constitutes assets just as important as the specimens or data that the instruments analyze. Historians of the HRST would not agree that printing out the documentation they created is a suitable preservation strategy, although they agree that it is better than no strategy at all. Sites at GMU and IATH, on the other hand, are what might be termed "thematic research collections." They are designed to support research and are structured, as Carole Palmer points out, to be open ended, flexible, and dynamic (Palmer 2003). These sites mix genres, formats, and secondary and primary sources, and all exist within a specific platform designed for querying and retrieval that is difficult to archive. These are not information resources that libraries have traditionally collected.

Therefore, it is possible to claim that an important feature of new-model scholarship is a blurring between "collections" and "services" and between research "information" and research "tools." An analog information resource such as a book represents a highly sophisticated technology for information transmission that does not depend on an array of peripheral technologies for use. The tools for mining information from a monograph, for example, include things embedded in the physical object, such as page numbers, indexes, tables of contents, typeface, spacing, and other formatting conventions. Save the book and you save the tools for search and retrieval.

In the digital realm, those search and retrieval tools are behaviors that are embedded in the software but are not, strictly speaking, the data themselves that are recorded in the digital object. Nonetheless, the tools or instruments needed to use the data must be conveyed with the digital objects. It is not beyond the reach of libraries to extend collection development paradigms to include the research tools and software interfaces along with the information; however, some preferred preservation strategies, such as migration, are fairly good at preserving the integrity of data but not the functionality of a digital object. Digital librarians need to know whether and when an information object includes the tools and behaviors, as well as the data, and policies must be developed that support those choices. Making custodial provisions for these types of digital resources also includes ensuring that subject specialists and selectors are trained to understand those tools.

## How Do We Sustain These Resources?

Another issue—sustainability—must be added to considerations of quality and appropriateness for acquisition. Librarians must not only assess the digital object's value for their institution but also determine whether the institution can sustain access to the object over time. Access involves many factors besides good storage and preservation: it includes creating metadata for preservation, search, and retrieval; maintaining hardware and software that can read the digital file; and providing reference help, among other things. Given the multiple (sometimes unquantifiable) costs of acquiring and maintaining Web-based scholarship, negotiations over acquisition between the library and the scholar often revolve around the perceived value of the object and soft projections about investments required to enable future use.

In many cases, the best both parties can do is to ensure that the digital file gets deposited in a repository, even if the repository can guarantee only that the bit stream will remain intact (physical preservation), as opposed to guaranteeing the logical rendering of the bits into an original digital object format over time (logical preservation). Because bit storage is possible and often not too expensive, this solution for physical preservation has much to recommend it, even if logical preservation of the digital object, needed for recalling the bits from storage and (re)creating the object, is an uncertainty. Inadequate as it may seem to some, it does trump total inaction and is in the spirit of experimenting, assessing, and learning as one goes.

The lack of clarity about the intended audience for or use of the digital objects creates problems for preservation as well as for selection. The strategy one chooses for preserving a digital object is usually calibrated to enable some future use; for example, cataloging (or metadata) choices always try to provide for scenarios in which a user will attempt to discover that object. Specifying the uses in the beginning goes a long way to ensuring the authenticity and reliability of the object; it is also of great use to an end user. As an ironic example of such forethought, the William Blake Archive has an agreement with the Charles Babbage Institute's Center for the History of Information Technology to preserve what IATH sees as the archival value of the site, that is, the textual record of how the site has been created, developed, and maintained. In this instance, the Blake Archive is seen to be significant as an early example of the use of digital technology for humanistic scholarship, fitting in well with the Babbage's collecting scope. Therefore, provision has been made to preserve that particular value of the archive, not the content of the archive itself. (This does not preclude preserving that content under different auspices.)

Better approaches to ensuring the accessibility of complex digital behaviors in the future entail engaging the creator in stipulating the intended use. Some digital artists, creating works that are essentially interactive, performative, or based on dynamic objects, are helping to ensure the authenticity of persistent objects by declaring what elements of the object are needed to re-create the experience of the art. These elements range from hardware specification (for example, a certain size and resolution of screen, or certain processing speeds but not others) to specific features of the software that must be replicable. (These declarations are often printed out on acid-free paper for archival purposes, an irony seldom lost on the artists.)

With complex digital objects, there is a disjunction between what scholars wish to create and hand off to a third party for preservation and what a given third party is willing to commit to preserving. There are ways to bridge that gap—for example, creators can fully document what their work is and which elements are most important to preserve or adhere to formats and markups that preservationists are able to manage. Developing good practice for creation, as well as preservation, is iterative and needs to be informed by research, testing, and analysis. It is important for all to take a long view of their work and to keep moving forward, one step at a time.

## ORGANIZATIONAL APPROACHES TO PRESERVING DIGITAL CONTENT

Digital preservation only begins with capturing and storing digital files; to ensure ongoing access to those files, someone must manage them continually. Media degradation and hardware/software dependencies pose risks to data over time. A critical first step is to consider the technical factors involved in managing these risks.[5] But preservation also requires developing business models for sustainable repository services; addressing intellectual property constraints that hamper archiving; creating standards for metadata; and training creators, curators, and users in appropriate technologies, among other things.[6]

Each community of creators and users of digital information has a stake in keeping digital files accessible. Each community must consider its responsibilities for ensuring the longevity of information it deems important. Many in the research community expect that libraries and archives—and, by extension, museums and historical societies—should bear the responsibility for preservation and access in the digital realm, just as they have in the analog. However, evidence abounds that these institutions, crucial as they are, cannot fulfill this responsibility alone.

It has been decades since scholars in the humanities held significant responsibility for developing or managing library collections. The post-World War II professionalization of librarianship, with the increasing specialization of academic disciplines, has tended to distance faculty from the stewardship of information resources on campus. There are notable exceptions, including the oral historians and ethnographers who document behaviors, gather evidence, and create collections. There are also a host of social sciences that depend on their practitioners to gather data and deposit them in community

5 See Appendix 2 for details.

6 See Appendix 1 for a discussion of the organizational issues important for digital archiving.

archives; one example of such an archives is the Inter-university Consortium for Political and Social Research (ICPSR). The digital transformation is quickly eroding the distance between scholar and custodian, and faculty members are being asked once again to assume roles in the creation, preservation, and dissemination of scholarly resources.

Faculty members are not alone in redefining the scope of their responsibilities in the digital realm. Libraries, publishers, and academic associations that are seriously engaging the challenges of digital preservation are finding themselves in roles that are in some respects unfamiliar. Significant experiments in digital preservation are under way in many arenas, as Greenstein, Smith, and Flecker point out in their essays (see Appendixes 1 and 2). Each effort is bounded by the interests of the participants, the constraints of present technologies, and a dearth of tested models for sustainability. Nonetheless, we have much to learn from them. Looking at the range of institutions and individuals engaged in digital preservation, it is perhaps most instructive to divide these models in two groups: those models developed by institutions or enterprises that address their own preservation needs; and those models developed by enterprises whose communities of participants cross institutional boundaries.

## Enterprise-Based Preservation Services

### Research Libraries

Several research libraries are preserving university-created digital assets. Most of the 124 libraries belonging to the Association of Research Libraries (ARL) create digital content, chiefly by converting analog texts and images they already hold in their collections. Of these, a smaller number say that they are managing or intend to manage those collections for long-term access (Library of Congress 2003). The caution captured by the word "intend" reflects the consensus in the library world that there is no way to guarantee ongoing access to digital assets in the same way we can analog. In the analog realm there is agreement about the best way to preserve print-on-paper sources; the challenge is not *how* to preserve, but how to do so *cost-effectively*. In the digital realm, however, no such agreed-upon standards exist, at least for the complex objects generated by humanities scholars.

Most relevant to the preservation of Web-based resources are the actions of a few large universities that are building repositories to preserve faculty output and, in some cases, student output.

**University of California Libraries (www.cdlib.org and lib.berkeley.edu).** The University of California (UC) Libraries are developing a digital preservation program under the aegis of the California Digital Library (CDL) that will serve the entire system of libraries and be distributed across all nine campuses. CDL is shaping itself to be the central node in the UC digital preservation network. Under this scenario, local nodes of the network—in campus libraries, research institutes and laboratories, and museums—can offer specific preservation services for local clientele while relying on the system-wide infrastructure to support common digital preservation needs, from metadata standards to linking services and persistent identifiers. Each campus can customize delivery of centrally held materials to its own users.

The university library system is active in areas that target specific user needs. Through its E-Scholarship program, it has begun taking in data created by the faculty to manage over time. This program is not prescriptive about what it will take; it sees itself as the place where faculty can deposit data sets, preprints, and other materials that fall outside the purview of a campus library. The CDL is also partnering with other universities and with the San Diego Super Computer Center to develop models for managing journal literature, government documents, museum objects, and other complex digital objects over time.

**DSpace at the Massachusetts Institute of Technology (MIT) (www.dspace.org).** Recently inaugurated at the MIT Libraries, DSpace is an institutional repository that will provide basic bit storage and digital object management delivery, primarily for MIT faculty research materials. It will develop a format registry specifying documentation and best practices for metadata. Faculty members may contribute content using DSpace's workflow submission system or contract with the library to process the intake. In collaboration with several research libraries across the country, DSpace is testing its software by conducting interoperability experiments. MIT plans to develop a federation of research libraries using the DSpace concept. It began to take in content at the end of 2002.

DSpace results from a collaboration between MIT and Hewlett Packard (HP) to develop an open-source turnkey system for digital asset management. HP is interested in developing and bringing to market a digital asset management system that works as easily with unstructured data as it does with structured. DSpace and HP are investigating ways to standardize content upon "ingest" (deposit into the repository) in ways that can be readily adapted by their federated partners. The team hopes to develop techniques for "personal archiving" so that faculty members can easily address issues of digital preservation when they create materials. Library managers believe that MIT faculty members are generally aware of the risk that threatens the longevity of their intellectual output and that they have an interest in working on a solution. Faculty members may be less aware of the complexity of finding that solution and the cost of implementing it over time. The MIT Libraries managers see DSpace as a way not only to address the preservation problem but also to engage faculty as partners in preservation.

MIT Libraries staff members are developing a business plan that includes a record of what it costs to run DSpace, and they hope to present possible revenue models. They expect the resulting models to be a combination of institutional funding and revenue-generating services, such as reformatting and creation of metadata. DSpace managers plan to accept whatever data faculty members are willing to deposit. At least, they will be able to return to the depositor the bits that were deposited. They are also specifying the file formats whose migration and management DSpace will support. Beyond that, they will do the best they can and hope to learn as much as they can from the experience. (Unlike UVA's IATH, the MIT Libraries are not committed to preserving software applications, only the content.)

**Harvard University Libraries (hul.Harvard.edu/ldi).** Harvard University Libraries take another approach to establishing a preservation repository. The libraries view digital preservation as the responsibility of many in the campus community, not just a few designated experts in the libraries. They believe that effective preservation will depend on technical and curatorial expertise found throughout the university. At Harvard, individual curators and libraries are responsible for selecting the material to be preserved. (The university has more than 100 libraries among its schools.) Digital content created outside the library system poses problems because standard documentation cannot be enforced at the time of creation, and normalizing all the content for deposit into the archive, when feasible, is usually too labor-intensive. In response to the problems presented by such heterogeneous file formats, the Harvard repository will provide three levels of service:

- service for normative formats that the repository will keep renderable
- service for formats for which the repository will keep the bits in order but will not take responsibility for keeping the files renderable
- service for all other, more complex, formats

**Stanford University Libraries (http://www-sul.stanford.edu/).** Stanford University Libraries (SUL) are building a digital repository that will take in any digital content that Stanford deems worthy of permanent preservation. The content will come from several sources: new digital conversion projects; so-called "legacy" digital content already owned by SUL; digital content purchased from external sources, including e-journals and e-texts; donations (such as archives); ongoing submissions, such as the Stanford Scholarly Communications Service, CourseWork (Stanford's OKI-based course management system); and metadata related to other SUL initiatives. Over time, Stanford hopes to offer preservation services to the publishers with whom it works through HighWire Press as well as to other off-campus partners.

Another digital preservation endeavor being developed is LOCKSS (Lots of Copies Keep Stuff Safe), a system based on the tried-and-true analog preservation strategy of redundancy. LOCKSS ensures that many digital systems in different locations across the continent and abroad retain caches of identical digital content. Now in beta test, LOCKSS enables institutions to create low-cost, persistent digital caches of authoritative versions of http-delivered content. With specially created software, institutions locally collect, store, preserve, and archive authorized content, thus safeguarding their communities' access to that content while doing no harm to publishers' business models. Although LOCKSS is now restricted to electronic journals, application to other genres is being explored. The software is distributed as open source.

In the period of transition to whatever digital preservation infrastructure will emerge, a major problem is that many scholars experimenting with the most innovative digital technology for research and teaching are not affiliated with major universities such as MIT or UC. On most campuses, if scholars were to turn to the library for help in preparing digital content so that the library could later acquire and preserve it, they might find the staff willing to help but without the means or the infrastructure to support the creation or preservation of digital scholarship.

### *Academic Disciplines*

Scholars who are not affiliated with a major university may be spared the prospect of major data loss because there are discipline-based approaches to archiving data. Examples include the Astrophysics Data System (ADS) and the ICPSR. What characterizes these fields is the quantity of data created and used, as well as the type. The data stored by the ICPSR, for example, are in fairly standard and highly structured formats. Information assets that are deemed important are normalized to improve the chances of their persistence. In fields that rely on massive data gathering and computer manipulation, such as genomics, researchers are required by their funders, as well as their own need for access, to deposit their data into a common database. The data must be submitted in formats upon which the community of depositors and users have agreed.

The contrast between these disciplines and those in the humanities is obvious. Humanistic inquiry is not characterized by teams of scholars, large grant support, or the creation of masses of new data for common use by the field. Even the largest and most robust of the humanities disciplines have learned societies that are not preserving, or planning to preserve, the born-digital resources that their own members create or rely on.

### *Publishers*

Publishers represent another group that is planning for the preservation of digital content. Some publishers that market to the academic community, such as Reed Elsevier, Oxford University Press, the American Physical Society (APS), and the American Geophysical Union (AGU), have committed to deliver digital access services to their core journals. Elsevier Science, for example, guarantees access to back publications for a certain period. This service is a business proposition for them. They offer their authors and subscribers a publication "of record" that can be cited and accessed in the future without users finding broken links. Such warrant of future citation is important for the academic system of reward and tenure. Other presses that aspire to manage their digital assets for long periods of time are developing in-house systems, though digital asset management systems are different from preservation. Publishers do not design their asset management systems to ensure the preservation of their digital publications in perpetuity, as illustrated by the recent controversy over Elsevier's deletion of some articles from its database (Foster 2003). Publishers that do wish to provide for such longevity have turned in some cases to libraries—APS is one—to host a mirror site or serve as a dark repository for fail-safe backup.

The AGU is an interesting model. It has complete control over the format in which it publishes and preserves, and it saves everything it publishes. The archive is set up as an independent legal entity, with an endowment that is empowered to manage the archival collection if AGU were to become defunct. The costs of preservation are borne by the readers, who pay a "tax" built into the subscription, and by authors, who pay per-page charges. The archive is not searchable, and it offers no user services. For security reasons, the collections will be copied worldwide. This will be done through arrangements with AGU's European counterpart and similar organizations. Significantly, AGU does not preserve any of the underlying data that provide the evidence cited in reports. Should scientists of the next century wish to view the data supporting a particular interpretation of, for example, a seismic event discussed in a journal article, they would not be able to do so. The article would be available, but its links to source data would no doubt be broken.

Over time, the loss of the source data may pose a more serious threat than loss of the interpretation of such data in the secondary literature, yet little attention is paid to this problem. As long as the secondary literature plays a decisive role in the promotion and tenure of faculty, scholars, their publishers, and their campus libraries will be motivated to find ways to preserve it. But what about preservation as a public trust? Who is responsible for looking beyond a profession's incentives for preservation to address the larger national and international need to preserve the data and primary sources that underlie scientific, technological, and scholarly advances? This would seem to be a national imperative that government preservation strategies can and should address, given that much of these data are built from federal grant-supported research.[7]

### Government-Sponsored Preservation

Government and state agencies have a legal mandate to maintain records and make them accessible to the public. Now that most government agencies are conducting their business electronically, that mandate is in jeopardy. The major collecting agencies of the federal government—the National Records and Archives Administration (NARA), the National Library of Medicine (NLM), and the National Agricultural Library (NAL)—have programs in place to research and develop electronic records creation and preservation. Their research

---

[7] This subject is identified as a vital part of the science and engineering cyberinfrastructure in National Science Foundation 2003, and National Science Board 2002.

and development agendas are crucially important to all citizens and should also be of benefit to the academic community. NARA's research work with the San Diego Supercomputer Center (SDSC) holds the promise of ensuring the future legibility of such structured documents as e-mails, though the Archives is just beginning to operationalize the research results, and the value of the SDSC research for building a scalable and sustainable digital archiving system is unknown. Part of the success of this work depends on the degree of control that a repository has over the file upon accessioning. Businesses and agencies are in a position to mandate the form that official documents are to take. Research libraries do not have that type of control over scholars and the other data creators they serve.

Only two government agencies, the Smithsonian Institution (SI) and the Library of Congress (LC), have collecting policies that include a large amount of the heterogeneous digital content under consideration here. (NLM and NAL collect technical and clinical materials that differ significantly from the special collections found in SI and LC.) Through its institutional archives, the Smithsonian has begun a program to preserve electronic records, and in some cases institutional Web sites, across the many entities that are part of the SI. However, none of the SI museums, such as the National Museum of American History, which collects important archives in the history of American invention, has begun to acquire Web-based sources as original sources, and none plans to do so.

The Library of Congress, which receives mandatory deposits of copyrighted works through its Copyright Office, has begun to collect contemporary works in digital formats, including Web sites and materials captured from the Web. More important, through a congressional mandate enacted in 2000, the National Digital Information Infrastructure and Preservation Program (NDIIPP), LC received an appropriation of up to $100 million to develop, design, and implement a preservation infrastructure that would create the technical, legal, organizational, and economic means to enable a variety of preservation stakeholders to work collaboratively to ensure the persistence of digital heritage (Library of Congress 2003). LC has proposed that such sectors as higher education, science, and other academic and research enterprises take primary responsibility for collecting, curating, and ensuring the preservation of their own information assets, especially those that are not deposited for copyright protection. The national infrastructure would enable preservation among many actors by engendering agreement on standards, ensuring that intellectual property laws encourage rather than deter preservation and access for educational purposes, and facilitating the building and certification of trusted repositories in a networked environment.

As part of this proposed infrastructure, LC has developed a preliminary technical architecture that would be built to serve as the backbone for a national infrastructure for digital preservation. This distributed architecture starts from the premise that the core functions of libraries and archives, from acquisition to user services, should be disaggregated in a networked environment. It does not envision that every collecting institution would assume the burden of building and maintaining digital preservation repositories; rather, it foresees that a handful of trusted repositories in higher education, such as those discussed above, will be certified through some means to assume a national responsibility for preservation. This scenario also envisions that major creators and users of digital information, such as research universities, would have repositories to manage their own digital output, at least for short-term needs. These repositories would differ from archival repositories because their primary purpose would be to facilitate access and dissemination, not to guarantee fail-safe preservation (see pp. 27-28).

For research universities, publishers, academic disciplines, and government agencies, the incentive to preserve digital materials is to protect institutional or proprietary information assets for future use or, in the case of the government bodies, to comply with legal requirements. Preservation is central to the core values of each enterprise. The types of preservation each undertakes—be it short-term asset management for publishers, preservation "in perpetuity" for universities whose mission is to further the creation of knowledge, or records management and selected permanent retention of government records by archives—is shaped by the enterprise and its mission.

## Community-Based Preservation Services

What happens to the scholarship created and primary source data collected outside the handful of universities and scientific disciplines that commit to preservation and dedicate resources to support it? Most digital resources that scholars create today have no guarantee of surviving long enough to be acquired for long-term preservation and access by libraries, archives, or historical societies. What services are available to such collecting institutions to meet their own mission-driven goals of continuing to acquire and serve materials of research value that are born digital?

There are now no digital preservation service bureaus that can offer the full range of services needed by such libraries and archives (or creators, for that matter). Nonprofit membership organizations that have served libraries for decades, most notably the Online Computer Library Center (OCLC) and the Research Libraries Group, are developing a variety of preservation services for their members while also engaging in research on metadata standards and other topics that benefit the larger library community. Both organizations hope to develop services that their members not only need but also can and will pay for. The Center for Research Libraries, which has been a central repository for collecting, preserving, and providing access to important but little-used research collections, is also contemplating offering similar services to members for certain classes of digital materials.

### JSTOR (www.jstor.org)

JSTOR is an example of an archiving service with a business model that promises to be sustainable over time. JSTOR preserves and provides access to digital back files of scholarly journals in humanities, social sciences, and some physical and life sciences. This nonprofit enterprise, which began with a major investment of seed capital from a foundation, offers a service that is in growing demand. As a service organization, JSTOR is an interesting hybrid that reveals much about how various members of the research community perceive the value of preservation and access. JSTOR is a subscription-based enterprise that defines itself first and foremost as an archiving service. It charges a one-time fee to all subscribers to support the costs of digitizing print journals and managing those files. Many libraries subscribe to JSTOR because they want to offer their users electronic access to these journals, and they may place a much higher value on the access than on the preservation function of JSTOR. Because of the ways that library and university budgets work, most libraries probably pay for JSTOR from their acquisitions funds rather than from preservation budgets. This reality has the perhaps regrettable effect of further hiding from plain sight the costs of preserving analog and digital information resources and the crucial dependence of access on preservation.

It is not yet clear how preservation of digital scholarship will be paid for, or even how much it will cost, in the future, but it will be a cost that cannot be deferred or ignored. JSTOR managers have tried to keep this problem in the foreground and have been documenting what JSTOR usage can tell us about how access to digital secondary literature can affect research strategies and agendas. Much work remains, however, for digital service providers to be able to determine what such services cost, how much of a market they can make for such services, and whether any will offer the kinds of retail services needed by data creators working outside large and securely funded libraries.

### The Internet Archive (www.archive.org)[8]

Another model of preservation, the Internet Archive, merits consideration, in part because of its promise to capture passively (or at least in a largely automated manner) much of what is publicly available on the Web, including many scholar-produced sites under discussion. Since 1996, the Internet Archive has been storing crawls of the Web. It now contains about 250 terabytes, and is the largest publicly available collection on the Web. The broad and wide-ranging crawls it regularly conducts represent about 2 billion pages and cover 40 million sites. The Archive also has several targeted collecting programs that focus on one or more specific site profiles and often are designed to go into the so-called Deep Web for retrieval of complex or otherwise inaccessible sites. The Archive plans to make copies of its data to store elsewhere. It aspires, therefore, to secure physical

---

[8] The author thanks Raymie Stata of the Internet Archive for information about the Archive and its range of activities.

preservation of Web sites. It does not address the logical preservation that may be needed to search and retrieve complex digital objects over time.

Many people who use the Web, scholars included, see the Internet Archive as a "magic-bullet" solution to the archiving problem. They mistakenly believe that the Internet Archive crawls and preserves all parts of the World Wide Web. Although the Archive can harvest much of the publicly available surface Web, most of the Web is closed to the Archive's crawlers (Lyman 2002). Sites in the Deep Web that cannot be harvested by crawlers include databases (the sorts of materials that generate responses to queries made "on the fly"); password-protected sites, such as those that require subscription for use (*The Wall Street Journal*); and sites with robot exclusions (*The New York Times*). Few sites produced by academic institutions are likely to fall into the latter two categories, but many fall into the first. Although a Web crawl does not require the cooperation of the creator or publisher, and thus can capture staggering amounts of material, it does not regularly penetrate the Deep Web and cannot capture interactive features on the Web. (Parts of the Deep Web are accessible to crawling, though, because they are linked to "surface" sites.) These features pose problems for scholarly innovators who create in multimedia or build querying into their sites.

The World Wide Web has neither a center nor a periphery: it is decentralized and boundless. As the Web grows, the managers of the Archive are realizing that they must become selective in their acquisition of content. Indeed, the Internet Archive is approaching a stage that is familiar to the most ambitious and wide-ranging of collectors and collecting institutions—the stage where it is necessary to focus on a set, or subset, of the universe of the possible.

Brewster Kahle, the moving spirit behind the Archive, has a special interest in capturing the underdocumented aspects of contemporary life revealed on the Web. He is encouraging national libraries to reach an agreement to collect sites that originate within their borders, to increase coverage worldwide, and to reduce possible redundancies where they are undesirable. The National Library of Australia (NLA) has been collecting Australian Web sites on PANDORA (Preserving and Accessing Networked Documentary Resources of Australia) for some time. Although such collecting has been outside the framework of any international agreement, PANDORA has been closely watched to see how feasible the approach will be. It turns out that, because the NLA selects and checks for copyright clearances, collecting Web sites, even within a single country domain, is very labor-intensive.

Until recently, the Internet Archive focused on collecting sites. With the debut of the Wayback Machine, however, the Archive offers what one staff member calls "retail" access to the Web, allowing individual users to search for specific sites. The Archive sees a need to develop a library-like workbench of research tools that provide technical and programmatic interfaces to the archived collections at a high level of abstraction. Although the Archive sees itself sharing many values and functions of research libraries in terms of collecting and preserving, it distinguishes itself from them because of its special interest in being a center of innovation and experimentation and operating alongside—but outside—a larger institution such as a university.

The Internet Archive is supported by philanthropy, government grants, and some contracts for specific purposes, but its financial future is not guaranteed. The largest cost component is content acquisition, and the Archive insists that these costs, which are growing exponentially, must be reduced. The high cost of acquisition, incidentally, seems to be a characteristic feature of digital repositories, be they very inclusive, such as the Internet Archive, or relatively exclusive. The Arts and Humanities Database (AHDS) in the United Kingdom determined that a hefty 70 percent of its operating costs goes to acquisition, and most of the rest to access services. Preservation of bits (the "spinning of disks," as one former AHDS manager put it) has been only a small fraction of the total spending.

The Internet Archive's commitment to being freely accessible diminishes its opportunities for financial support from libraries or commercial entities. It often crawls material that is under copyright protection without seeking permission first. (It scrupulously follows a policy of removing access to sites on the Wayback Machine when asked to do so by the Web master of a site, however.) Although some have suggested that libraries can find at least one potent solution to collection and preservation by contracting with the Archive to collect on their behalf, or simply to support the Archive in its present activities, libraries must be daunted by the legal implications of the Archive's approach to capture. The Archive has successfully collected specific types of sites for the Library of Congress (on presidential elections, September 11, and others), but even the LC, which Congress mandated to acquire copyrighted materials through demand deposit, will have to seek a clear ruling about whether acquiring such sites through Web crawling is within the letter, not just the spirit, of copyright law.

What about the data that the Archive has already amassed? It may well share the fate of many an outstanding private collection and be passed, at some point during or after the collector's life, to an institution that can care for it indefinitely. The role of the private collector, who identifies and secures for posterity materials of great value that others somehow miss, is unlikely to diminish in the digital realm. Indeed, it is likely to increase.

## The Role of Funders in Digital Preservation

All the actors familiar in traditional library collecting have now appeared on the stage: the creators and the disciplines that support them, the publishers, the libraries, and the many services that support libraries. All have a stake in digital preservation, and all have distinctly new roles to play in the digital landscape. But what about funders—the foundations, university governing boards, and federal agencies that have played decisive roles in funding the creation and dissemination of scholarship?

Federal agencies have only recently begun to address the long-term access of digital materials whose creation they fund. The National Science Foundation (NSF), which has had a Digital Libraries Initiative (DLI) program in place for several years, has put more dollars behind the digital library research agenda than any other entity. It was not until last year, however, in response to a request by the LC, that the NSF made digital preservation a specific feature of its funding. The Digital Government Program, the DLI, and LC convened librarians and archivists, computer scientists, technologists, and government officials to develop a research agenda for digital preservation, and it intends to put out a call for proposals in 2003.

The other, more modestly funded, federal agencies that support digital library and content development—the Institute for Museum and Library Services (IMLS), NEH, and the National Endowment for the Arts (NEA)—all encourage their grant applicants to describe their plans to preserve the digital content they create. In so doing, they present sustainability as a competitive feature of a grant project. A commitment to preserve digital content is unlikely to become a grant requirement unless preservation services are available to chronically underfunded cultural heritage institutions. But encouraging applicants to plan for such preservation activities at least raises awareness of the need to think about the upkeep of digital assets among institutions that have traditionally focused more on the creation than the maintenance of content.

A handful of private foundations, including The J. Paul Getty Trust, The Andrew W. Mellon Foundation, and the Alfred P. Sloan Foundation, have funded the creation of digital scholarship. Because of their focus on research and scholarship, these foundations have an interest in ensuring that solutions to the digital preservation problem are found sooner rather than later, and they are thus seeking ways to use their influence to help. As long as preservation appears to be mainly a technical problem, foundations may not identify an active role for themselves. But as has been shown, technology is just one of several challenges to preserving digital content. The Mellon Foundation, for example, has funded the development and assessment of business models that would make preservation a sustainable enterprise. The Foundation's involvement began with JSTOR, but has extended to several other initiatives already under way, such as DSpace, and to partnerships between publishers and libraries to preserve e-journal content. By encouraging innovative and responsible behaviors, all funders that support higher education can help define the crucial role the scholar must play in preserving digital scholarship.

Some funders incorporate preservation and its costs into their grants. For example, the Arts and Humanities Research Board and the National Environmental Research Council in Great Britain not only require that grantees deposit their data into a central databank but also make the creators "pay" for archiving their materials by incorporating preservation into the data creation grant (usually 2 percent to 6 percent of the grant). The archeological community in the United States follows a similar practice, where the commercial entities developing a site tend to pay for preservation. This model can be extended to other disciplines and to other funding agencies (such as ADS, ICPSR, and GenBank, the human genome databank) when data deposit is feasible.

Higher education administrators and governing boards, important sources of funding for the creation and preservation of scholarship, have remained curiously distanced from this issue. Some institutions have made funding both digital scholarship and librarianship campus priorities—the University of Virginia and Harvard University come to mind—but these are the noteworthy exceptions. Seldom have campus executives articulated a vision for the stewardship of university information assets, despite the importance of digital information networks on their campuses.

Campus administrators at the California Institute of Technology are an exception. They have spoken out on the institution's obligation to preserve and make available the output of the faculty, both in the interest of furthering science and to share with taxpayers the fruits of government investment in science. However, although an institutional repository has been up and running for some time, the volume of contributions from faculty members has been small (Young 2002). It is important to identify the barriers to deposit in this case, for they may suggest how incentives for deposit can be created.

Intellectual property issues around access loom large in the sciences, and that may help explain why it is difficult to get scientists to contribute to institutional archives that are publicly available. DSpace may be instructive in this area, as it will have to allow depositors to remove articles if needed to comply with a given publisher's mandate. DSpace will, however, retain a record of the article having once been a part of the repository.

Workflow issues are and will be a major barrier to deposit of scholarly resources into preservation repositories, as the example of HRST shows. If there were a frictionless way to create documents in preservation-friendly formats and to send the files to a repository for safe keeping with the click of a mouse, all without distracting creators from their primary focus, we might see different behaviors emerge. The possibility of automating key aspects of creating preservation-friendly formats, genres, and metadata should rise to the top of the research and funding agendas for research-intensive institutions. This could be one result of a commitment by senior campus administrators to the stewardship of digital information.

## MOVING FORWARD

In the short term, there are several actions that are within reach for both data creators and data repositories that will advance the preservation agenda. For the creators, these actions include the following:
- Work with libraries when beginning a project

- Use standard and, when possible, nonproprietary formats
- Declare the intended use and audience
- Declare intended longevity

For the repositories, such actions include the following:
- Work with data creators during all phases of the creation
- Declare policies and capabilities for archiving differing formats
- Take materials into custody for preservation experiments

Beyond these actions, digital scholars should think deeply about developing an informatics for their discipline, as has happened in some data-intensive sciences, so that they are able to create digital objects that share vocabularies and descriptive markup, facilitate shared access to information resources, and allow ready repurposing for teaching and scholarship. Teachers should ensure that their students master the skills needed to use the new technologies. Instruction in digital information literacy and research skills should be as vital a part of a student's training as is teaching how to work in primary sources or cite authorities appropriately. Research divisions of the learned societies can provide leadership in this area.

Libraries can initiate partnerships with scholars on campus and with learned societies and their publishers to share knowledge and agree on common approaches to data creation and preservation. They can develop transparent digital preservation policies and make them accessible on their Web sites. They can develop depository programs that promise not necessarily to preserve flawlessly in perpetuity but rather to partner with data depositors in experiments that take in formats favored by disciplines and knowledge communities, perform risk assessments on those file formats, explore approaches that reduce format vulnerabilities, and share the results of that work with other data communities.

## Looking Ahead

The current lack of provision for the responsible creation, curation, and retention of research data is highlighted in the National Science Foundation's report on the science and engineering information infrastructure, which addresses the promise of computing capabilities to transform even further and more radically the conduct of basic and applied research (NSF 2003). This report has implications not only for scientific and engineering data; a similar argument could be mounted for the creation, curation, and preservation of nonscientific research data. There is no agency in the humanities with a mission, funding, or standing comparable to that of the National Academy of Sciences. The opportunities for articulating the problem of preserving nonscientific research data are therefore fewer, and, even when persuasive arguments are made, there are far fewer resources to commit to finding and funding solutions.

There are many barriers to digital preservation at this early stage in the development of digital information technologies, but they can be summed up in one phrase: lack of infrastructure. In the academy, and especially within humanities faculties, many scholars, teachers, and students will continue to look to libraries and archives to lead preservation efforts and to make information of high research value available now and into the future. The well-known preprint archive for high-energy physics, arXiv.org, moved from its home at a laboratory in Los Alamos to Cornell University because the lab did not see maintaining a historical record for access in the future as part of its mission. Even as the perception of the library's value for providing access to information is declining among some on campuses, the value that faculty place on the preservation function of libraries remains high (JSTOR 2002).

The research community must begin to grapple seriously with the nature of resources stewardship in the digital age. What worked in the analog realm might not work as well in the future. One perspective in the heated debate on electronic academic publishing holds that the technology allows radical changes in the creation and distribution of scholarship. Others sense that while technology creates opportunities for doing business better (for example, lowering publishing and distribution costs), it also has many disadvantages (the expenses of creating in standard formats and preservation are two big ones). Some libraries are trying to become points of dissemination for scholarly literature in a way that differs radically from their role in the distribution system of print resources.

Libraries, particularly their special collections and archives units, have been the traditional custodians of primary sources, and it is natural to expect that they should continue to play that role. However, while libraries and archives have the curatorial expertise needed to fulfill their roles in the digital arena, they generally lack the technical infrastructure to support the key functions of digital preservation. There is some debate about whether it is advisable, or even possible, for every institution in higher education, or even the largest institutions, to develop the full range of services needed for digital preservation. (For commonly agreed-upon minimum standards for long-term repositories, see Appendix 2.) The digital librarians and archivists who are most deeply engaged in building repositories and preservation services agree that repositories are difficult and expensive to build and maintain. They argue cogently that such repositories will be few and will serve many users, including other libraries. In a distributed network, there do not need to be many.

Others argue that every major university can and should have its own digital repository, although the reasons adduced for having one usually relate more to intellectual property matters surrounding publication than to long-term preservation. A white paper commissioned by the Scholarly Publishing and Academic Resources Coalition (SPARC) expands on one type of repository, designed to be "a component in a restructured scholarly publishing model . . . [and] . . . tangible embodiment of institutional quality" (Crow 2002). The paper advocates for institutional repositories to transform scholarly publishing by allowing libraries to compete with commercial publishers online, and to increase the prestige of the university and build brand identity by showcasing the intellectual property of its faculty. The paper suggests that the disaggregation of functions in the networked environment allows libraries to develop consortia to build and maintain repositories for any number of purposes, including preservation. The SPARC model of repository is, however, intended to be complemented by repositories that do stake a claim for preservation. A reliable chain of referencing in scholarly publishing and the promise of scholarship's persistence into the future are indispensable for the progress of science and humanities.

One challenge that remains is what happens to those scholarly resources created outside the purview of a large, well-funded research institution with a preservation mandate, such as those seated at the Dibner Institute and George Mason University. These resources share many of the characteristics of other noncommercial assets (or commercially produced assets that have exhausted their profitability) that can quickly become orphans in the world. In this way, they share the fate of most special collections.

Regardless of how this debate turns out, it is clear from the viewpoint of systems design that a robust network of repositories and services for long-term preservation of digital library objects favors a disaggregation of functions and does not require that each preserving institution have its own bit repository. The distributed architecture of preservation that LC proposes in its NDIIPP plan is one that will encourage even the smallest preservation and curatorial institutions to participate because it will allow them to bring their particular expertise to bear on some aspect of stewardship but not require that they replicate all aspects of preservation from bit repository to collections and end-user services. Such a system will address one need already apparent in the digital realm: the need to have in place an infrastructure that will allow both an aggressive rescue function to save endangered information assets and the ability to serve individual institutions, no matter the size, that are conscientious custodians of their digital collections.

## The Responsibility for Stewardship

How will we pay for such an infrastructure, and how do we move beyond the incentives born of enlightened self-interest that we see in institutions managing their own information assets?

In the long run, digital technology will force all engaged in the research enterprise—from university president to graduate student, from library director to reference librarian—to rethink stewardship. Like all big challenges, the debate about information stewardship in this transformed landscape should begin with a simple proposition: Everyone who has a stake in access to digital information has a stake in the preservation of digital data. In higher education, that means the debate would be joined by all, with discussions taking place across and among campuses.

It is a debate in which university and college administrators and governors must play a visible role. In many ways, the issue of preservation—of the long-term care of information assets whether or not they have commercial potential or are crucial for lucrative or well-funded areas of research—is the dark side of the debate raging on campuses about scholarly communication, or, to be more precise, about publishing. But underlying the integrity and value of published scientific and scholarly literature are the deep and broad expanses of unpublished data and primary sources on which scientific and humanistic inquiry are based. To continue investing heavily in creating digital information assets without shoring up their long-term accessibility is like building castles on sand.

Today, we can expect that institutions will pay more attention to securing their own information assets into the future, even if that means using outside preservation services. We can press learned societies and the scholarly disciplines they represent to declare and act on their responsibilities to the information sources crucial to their own work. We can ask that all members of the research community not only look after their own near-term interests but also take the long view of the resources on which their professions depend. In the end, this debate affects not only research institutions and their constituents but also the public at large. It is the public that supports a vast research enterprise through federal tax structures that subsidize foundations and private as well as public educational institutions. Those tax structures and the stream of funding that goes into research through federal agencies have been created because our country's Founders believed that the creation and dissemination of information and knowledge will lead to progress in the arts and sciences. It is not just digital information that is at risk if the academy does not act. It is also the compact between the public and the research-and-development infrastructure that the public supports.

## REFERENCES AND WEB SITES

*Web addresses were current as of March 10, 2003*

Crow, Raym. 2002. The Case for Institutional Repositories: A SPARC Position Paper. Washington, D.C.: The Scholarly Publishing & Academic Resources Coalition. Available at: www.arl.org/sparc/IR/ir.html.

Foster, Andrea L. 2003. Elsevier's Vanishing Act. *The Chronicle of Higher Education* (January 10). Available at: http://chronicle.com/free/v49/i18/18a02701.htm.

JSTOR. 2002. Faculty Response and Attitudes Toward Electronic Resources. Available at: www.jstor.org/news/2002.03/SurveyMarch2002.html.

Library of Congress. 2003. Preserving Our Digital Heritage. Plan for the National Digital Information Infrastructure and Preservation Program. Washington, D.C. Available at: www.digitalpreservation.gov.

Lyman, Peter. 2002. Archiving the World Wide Web. Building a National Preservation Strategy. Issues in Digital Media Archiving. Washington, D.C.: Council on Library and Information Resources. Available at: www.clir.org/pubs/reports/pub106/contents.html.

National Science Board. 2002. Science and Engineering Infrastructure for the 21st Century. (NSB 02-190). Draft dated December 4, 2002. Washington, D.C.: National Science Board. Available at: www.nsf.gov/nsb/documents/2002/nsb02190/nsb02190.doc.

National Science Foundation. 2003. Revolutionizing Science and Engineering through Cyberinfrastructure: Report of the National Science Foundation Blue-Ribbon Advisory Panel on Cyberinfrastructure. Washington, D.C.: National Science Foundation. Available at: www.communitytechnology.org/nsf_ci_report/.

Palmer, Carole L. Forthcoming. Thematic Research Collections. *Blackwell's Companion to Digital Humanities*, Autumn 2003.

Young, Jeffrey. 2002. "Superarchives" Could Hold All Scholarly Output. *The Chronicle of Higher Education*. July 5, 2002. Available at: http://chronicle.com/weekly/v48/i43/43a02901.htm#superarchive.

### Web Site References

9/11. http://911digitalarchive.org

Blake Archive. www.blakearchive.org

California Institute of Technology. http://library.caltech.edu/digital

DSpace at the Massachusetts Institute of Technology. https://hpds1.mit.edu/index.jsp

Harvard Library Digital Initiative. http://hul.Harvard.edu/ldi

Internet Archive. www.archive.org

JSTOR. www.jstor.org

Library of Congress. www.digitalpreservation.gov

LOCKSS. http://lockss.stanford.edu/projectstatus.htm

Monuments and Dust. www.iath.virginia.edu/mhc

My History Is America's History. www.myhistory.org/yourstories

Perseus. www.perseus.tufts.edu

Rossetti Archive. http://jefferson.village.virginia.edu/rossetti/

Stanford University Libraries. http://www-sul.stanford.edu/

University of California Libraries. http://library.berkeley.edu; and www.cdlib.edu.

# APPENDIX 1

# Organizational Models for Digital Archiving

*Dale Flecker*
*Harvard University Library*
*March 2002*

## Background

Before considering some of the organizational models that have emerged for the archiving of digital scholarly information, it is useful to step back and look at some factors that influence which organizations are likely to become active in this arena. These factors include the following:

*What organizations believe that digital archiving is their role?*
Digital archiving is complex and costly, and it requires a long-term institutional commitment. Traditionally, few institutions have assumed the role of preserving resources over long periods of time: such institutions have included research and national libraries, records and manuscript archives, museums, and entities interested in documenting their own history. Archiving is not a responsibility assumed lightly. In general, preservation is undertaken by institutions for which it is an explicit part of their social role and a need or expectation of the population they serve.

*What organizations have the infrastructure needed for digital archiving?*
Digital archiving is a technically complex task and requires a fair amount of infrastructure: appropriate hardware and software, a sound and secure environment, and skilled staff. The increasing capacity and ease of use of desktop or office-level technology may at first glance make infrastructure seem to be less important than it once was; however, the increasing scale of material to be archived, and continual technological change, make the need for a robust and professional infrastructure ever more important. The need for infrastructure has been a factor to date in keeping many smaller, less technically sophisticated institutions from extending their collections to include digital resources. Over time, however, the need for technical infrastructure may become the least important of the factors listed here, because commercial service bureaus such as the incipient OCLC digital archive may be available to handle the technical aspects of archiving.

*Who has the right to archive digital information?*

Most digital information is owned by someone. The ease with which we daily access an enormous range of resources over the Internet masks the core question of intellectual property rights. Some materials we access are under explicit licenses (libraries now have experts who spend their days negotiating such licenses), and most of these licenses clearly state what rights an institution has to locally store and manipulate the resource. Archiving as we generally think of it would not be permitted under most contemporary use licenses.

Other materials are provided over the Internet without explicit license. However, the fact that there is no access barrier does not mean there is no archiving barrier. The "free" material on the Internet may be even more challenging for archiving than licensed resources are. Because there is no explicit negotiation over these materials, there is no opportunity for an archive to negotiate the necessary rights.

In most cases, legal archiving requires an explicit, voluntary relationship between the archive and the intellectual property owner. A possibly important exception is the legal provision for copyright deposit in many countries. National legislation varies as to whether digital materials are covered under mandatory copyright deposit, but there is a growing awareness of the need to provide such coverage. As time passes, national copyright libraries may have a legal advantage in building archival collections.

*Who can afford archiving?*

Archiving requires significant resources. Institutions that assumed an archival role in the paper era may not have the resources to do so in the digital domain. More than in the physical environment, digital collections require continual resource spending to keep them vital. Many physical collections have persisted despite years of neglect. The digital realm, however, is characterized by continual, rapid technological change. Unless investments are made regularly to move materials from platform to platform, and from format to format, older resources will become unreadable or unusable.

One important economic factor is whether much of the costly infrastructure required for archiving is already in place and supported as part of an institution's general operating environment and required by the institution's mission. Building archiving over such existing infrastructure can significantly reduce costs.

*Whom does the affected community trust?*

Archiving is not a disconnected activity; it is intended to support specific purposes for specific audiences. The questions of who should be an archive and what intellectual property gets deposited in an archive are frequently influenced by whom the target user community trusts. If the user community does not trust the competence, values, and viability of the archive, the necessary social support for the archiving activity may be missing.

## Organizational Models

At least five organizational models for archives of scholarly digital materials are commonly in use today.

### Discipline-Based Models

A specific discipline often has the primary interest and motivation to preserve research resources. For this reason, it is natural that archives are sometimes created within discipline-based organizations. Two examples of such discipline-based archives are

- The Inter-university Consortium for Political and Social Research (ICPSR): Housed at the Institute for Social Research at the University of Michigan, the ICPSR collects survey and economic data sets for use by social scientists. Its primary sources of data are the Bureau of the Census and other government agencies and individual scholars or research projects. The consortium takes responsibility for preserving deposited data sets and, depending on the likely importance of a data set, may invest in documentation and reformatting data for ease of use. The current collection contains about 3,500 studies. Access to the collection is generally limited to member institutions.
- The Astrophysics Data System (ADS): ADS collects and indexes the literature of astronomy. It is housed at the Harvard-Smithsonian Center for Astrophysics. The collection includes both retrospective literature (much of it digitized by the ADS back to volume 1 of any collected periodical) and prospective publications. An extensive system of links connects the ADS to other online information resources. The ADS has indexed about 2.5 million records. The scanned literature archive contains about 260,000 articles with a total of 1.9 million pages. The indexes and much of the collection of ADS are available to the public, but some of the recent materials can be accessed only by persons with subscriptions through the original publishers.

Both of these archives were purposely built within their respective disciplines using significant government funding. Both have become core resources within their disciplines: most researchers know about these archives and use their collections regularly, and it is widely expected that these collections will persist and grow. This expectation is a key strength of the discipline-based model; it encourages participation and provides the validation important to funding sources. In the case of ICPSR, any respectable scholar is expected to deposit data sets when his or her research on a given subject is finished; in fact, some funders make eventual deposit of data sets in ICPSR a condition of funding. This practice allows others to replicate analyses as part of the normal scholarly process of validation and to reuse the data for other analyses. Astronomers commonly expect that all journals in the field will cooperate with ADS, so that researchers can count on finding the relevant literature by searching one system. All relevant journals do cooperate, although some insist that users be connected to the journal's own site to access articles, rather than have the content served from the ADS.

ICPSR and ADS are funded differently. As a membership organization, ICPSR receives much of its core operational funding through member institution subscriptions. If an institution subscribes, its researchers and students can get copies of all data sets and associated documentation. ICPSR continues to receive federal funding for some of its activities. ADS is largely supported by the National Aeronautics and Space Administration (NASA).

### Commercial Services

There are domains where resources important to scholars are viable as commercial products. Examples are JSTOR and LexisNexis.

- JSTOR is a nonprofit company that provides access to digitized versions of major journals in several topic areas. It is licensed by nearly 1,300 colleges and universities, two-thirds of which are in the United States. In some disciplines (particularly the social sciences), JSTOR has become a core resource that is heavily used by scholars and students.

- LexisNexis has built an enormous collection of digital materials, mainly in law, business, and contemporary affairs. It is largely oriented toward use by law firms and businesses and derives most of its income from those markets, although it is also heavily used by universities. Essentially all the materials used for the study of contemporary American law are available from LexisNexis, and it is the single most widely used digital resource provided by academic libraries.

The advantage of commercial collections is that they answer the key question of how to financially support digital collections. It is the willingness of the commercial and legal communities to pay substantial fees for information access that makes LexisNexis viable; sales to the academic and research community could never generate enough income to support this costly collection. Another advantage of the commercial model is that, because the services must compete in the marketplace, they have a significant incentive to continue to add new content and functionality to their products. Both JSTOR and LexisNexis provide high functionality and attractive services. The down side of this need for added value is that the companies require significant capital investment. (In the case of JSTOR, this came from The Andrew W. Mellon Foundation.)

Because commercial services generally require payment for access, they are to some degree based on a model of scarcity: not everyone has access, because not everyone can pay. For scholarly purposes this is unfortunate, because it is in the interest of scholarship to have materials as widely available as possible.

Another issue central to the commercial model is that the intellectual property issues inherent in almost any collection of digital resources become more pronounced than they are in other models. When an organization is going to make money by use of someone else's intellectual property, licensing negotiations become a core activity. JSTOR and LexisNexis show the effect of such issues. The

LexisNexis collection has experienced continual turmoil in nonlegal materials, as content owners regularly change their minds about whether to allow distribution through the LexisNexis system. JSTOR has also had difficult issues in licensing content, and the publishers of many journals for which JSTOR provides retrospective content will not allow the inclusion of more recent digital materials, which the journals themselves are providing online.

An important issue associated with commercially supported research collections is continuity. What happens to the collection if the marketplace changes and the supporting service is no longer economically viable? LexisNexis is so central to the contemporary law community that this seems an unlikely possibility, at least at this point. In the case of JSTOR, however, the issue is real enough that an endowment has been established to provide for ongoing preservation of and access to the collection in the event of commercial failure.

### Government Agencies

Governments, particularly national governments, frequently support significant digital collections. National libraries, national archives, and scientific arms of government are most commonly the agencies involved. Two examples are

- PubMed Central: PubMed Central is a service of the National Library of Medicine. It provides access to and archiving for a variety of electronic journals in medicine. One of the aims of this system is to make access to new biomedical literature open to all in less than a year of its publication.
- PANDORA (Preserving and Accessing Networked Documentary Resources of Australia): The aim of PANDORA, a project of the National Library of Australia, is to collect, preserve, and give public access to Internet resources created in Australia. It is intended to fulfill the Library's traditional role of ensuring the continuing availability of "a comprehensive record of Australian history and creative endeavour" in the age of the Internet.

Although government agencies can be subject to cycles of funding growth and contraction, they also can command a level of resources not readily available to nonprofit institutions in the private sector. Archiving and providing access to resources is frequently a core mission for government agencies, particularly in documenting national history and accomplishments in science, culture, and technology.

Because of their prestige, social role, and credibility, governments can provide a comparatively stable base for archiving. National libraries are uniquely able to attract content contributions from a wide variety of corporate and noncorporate entities. Many national libraries also expect national copyright laws to evolve to cover the required deposit of digital materials, providing them with a tool for acquiring content that might otherwise be unavailable because of concerns about intellectual property rights.

One potential concern about government-based collections is that they may have an ideological or political bias. Governments frequently have specific views of history or culture that they wish either to promote or to suppress, and these views can influence what is collected. Sensitivities to political influence can also affect the collecting of unpopular or "unacceptable" materials (for example, pornography, neo-Nazi or other hate literature, or documents relating to pedophilia or euthanasia).

### Research Libraries

Research libraries are expanding their traditional role of collection building into digital materials. Two interesting examples of digital research collections in libraries, both of which are available at no charge to the public, are

- DSpace: This is a project of the Massachusetts Institute of Technology (MIT) Libraries that was developed with support from Hewlett-Packard. Described as a "digital archive to capture and distribute the intellectual output of MIT faculty," DSpace was originally envisioned as a collection of electronic preprints and journal articles. Today, the scope of this archive is widening to encompass research data and course-related materials.
- arXiv: arXiv is a large collection of digital preprints and journal articles, mainly in areas of physics and mathematics. Created by a physicist at the Los Alamos National Laboratory a decade ago, it has become a basic working tool and communication channel in some areas of physics. Responsibility for arXiv recently moved from Los Alamos to the Cornell University Library.

Collecting and providing access to research materials is core to the mission of research libraries. The question of mission was part of the motivation for transferring arXiv from the Los Alamos National Laboratory to the Cornell University Library: Los Alamos did not consider the support of a collection of research materials for the general physics and mathematics community central to its mission; Cornell did.

Research libraries provide the stable home that is appropriate for materials of persistent value. These libraries have expertise in collection building, access, and preservation. Most are beginning to build local infrastructures for housing and preserving digital resources; for instance, MIT is assuming that the DSpace infrastructure will serve as a base for other digital resources. Libraries also frequently have good relationships with the scholars who create many research resources. Because the libraries have a high level of credibility, scholars do not hesitate to trust them to protect and preserve materials.

DSpace is a leading example of what is likely to be a growing role for libraries in collecting and preserving digital resources created within their universities. There is growing awareness among scholars about the inherent fragility of digital materials. As scholars and their universities seek a locus for the maintenance of their digital assets, libraries are a natural choice.

### The Passionate Individual

Many great collections, particularly those of rare and ephemeral materials, have been the creation of individuals with a passionate interest in an area. To some degree, such collecting has continued in the digital era. Current archives, both of which are freely available to the public, include the following:

- The Internet Archive: This archive was conceived and built by Brewster Kahle, a computer scientist. It gathers and stores Web pages, mainly through cyclical "crawls" of the entire Internet. The collection, composed primarily of textual Web pages, already includes more than 100 terabytes of data and is growing at a rate of about 100 gigabytes a day.

- The David Rumsey Historical Map Collection: This is a collection of eighteenth-, nineteenth-, and twentieth-century North and South American cartographic materials digitized from the collection of businessman David Rumsey. It includes about 6,500 items from Rumsey's collection of 150,000. Rumsey collaborated with a specialized software firm to expand the ability of its software to handle cartographic materials.

It is extremely difficult to generalize about initiatives created by one individual. Each project reflects the topical passion, financial resources, technical skills and environment, and ability to inspire others to help in the effort of its initiator. Rumsey is working slowly, on a relatively small scale, with the technology vendor Luna Imaging. The Internet Archive has attracted much interest and support among technology companies, libraries, collectors, and other individuals intrigued by Kahle's vision, and it is growing at a dramatic rate. The archive is based on its founder's technical knowledge and expertise and on a cooperative arrangement with a technology company also owned by Kahle.

The sort of Web page collecting being done by the Internet Archive was widely discussed by others before this service began. The need to act fast to save some of the ephemeral documentation of our time that lived only on the Web was widely recognized, but institutions were reluctant to get involved because of their concern about intellectual property issues. The scale of the issue immobilized most; others, such as PANDORA, collected slowly because of the costs associated with obtaining clearing rights. The Internet Archive was willing to plunge ahead and assume the risk of copyright violation to ensure that the materials would not be lost.

Personally based digital archives are still new; it is not possible to predict how they will fare with time. It is possible that they will follow the path of many parallel collections of the paper era and, as time passes and those who started them grow older, will begin to look for institutional homes that can provide stable environments. On the other hand, the Internet Archive has attracted considerable outside support and might well represent a new type of specialized player in the archiving environment—one with a particular technological and resource-type niche that suits a given domain of materials. The Internet Archive has begun to provide project support to the Library of Congress, and the idea of making it an agent of the Library and assigning it responsibility for Web archiving in its area of expertise has been discussed.

## Summary

The examples of digital archives given in this paper vary enormously in the scope of their ambitions and collections, their motivations, the impetus for their creation, and their institutional settings, intended audiences, and funding sources. This is not surprising; traditional collecting institutions also varied a fair amount. There may well be other types of players in the digital arena. There are few commercial or discipline-based traditional collections analogous to LexisNexis or ADS. As digital information grows ever more central to various communities, the opportunity and need for archiving activities become more obvious, and the field attracts new players. Because we are only at the beginning of the digital era, this heterogeneity is likely to grow.

### *Web Site References*

arXiv: http://arxiv.org/
Astrophysics Data System: http://adswww.harvard.edu/
David Rumsey Historical Map Collection: http://
   www.davidrumsey.com/
DSpace: http://www.dspace.org/
ICPSR: http://www.icpsr.umich.edu/
Internet Archive: http://www.archive.org/
JSTOR: http://www.jstor.org/
LexisNexis: http://www.lexisnexis.com/
Pandora: http://pandora.nla.gov.au/
PubMedCentral: http://www.pubmedcentral.nih.gov/

## APPENDIX 2

# Digital Preservation in the United States:
## Survey of Current Research, Practice, and Common Understandings

*Daniel Greenstein, Digital Library Federation*
*Abby Smith, Council on Library and Information Resources*
*March 2002*

Libraries and archives have long preserved significant parts of the published and unpublished record. They do this to ensure that the information in those records will be available to those who need it. Preservation has always been seen as a necessary condition for access. When information is recorded on paper and other analog media, the major challenges to preservation are posed by the fragility of the medium and by the costs of providing suitable storage, which are often high.

In the United States, preservation has traditionally been a distributed activity. Each library or archives is responsible for maintaining the accessibility of its own holdings, for its own users. Together, these individual collections constitute the national collection. The materials have traditionally been used on-site, although they may be loaned to other institutions through lending agreements that are designed, in part, to protect the artifact being lent. Sharing of resources occurs through reformatting (onto microforms, through preservation photocopying, and so forth). But in each case, the physical artifacts are assets that belong to the library or archives. The information in these artifacts may or may not belong to the institution; in fact, rarely are intellectual property rights given to the repository in which the materials are held. In the analog realm, fulfilling preservation responsibilities has entailed both meeting the information needs of (mostly onsite) users and protecting institutional assets. Preservation responsibilities are assumed upon the acquisition of a physical item and they continue through its life cycle.

These interests—preservation, physical possession or ownership, and access—are seldom as allied in the digital realm as they are in the world of analog media. The function of preservation for the purpose of providing physical or intellectual access does not fall automatically to an institution through the agency of physical ownership. The stakeholders in digital preservation often come from the same sectors as do stakeholders in the analog realm. They include creators, distributors or publishers, repositories or libraries and archives, and users. But these stakeholders may play very different roles in the digital realm than they do in the analog realm—roles that can put them in conflict with one another in areas where their interests once were parallel. Digital stakeholders can also create new alliances of interests.

One critical challenge to digital preservation in the near term is technical: the rapid rate at which hardware and software become obsolete means that information written in a specific code to run on specific hardware may be stranded by the adoption of newer, better code and hardware. This is the problem facing individuals who want to read an early version of a Lotus 1-2-3 spreadsheet that they have on a 5-1/4-inch disk they used to run on an IBM PC. The implication is that decisions about selection for preservation that can be deferred in the analog realm must be addressed early in the life cycle of digital files.

This paper summarizes activities under way in the United States that are designed to address the variety of preservation challenges—technical, legal, and social—and the changing roles and responsibilities of preservation stakeholders. It is divided into the following major sections:

- *Common understandings among stakeholders* describes the agreements that exist among those who take an interest in the long-term management of digital information.
- *Practical preservation activity* reports real archiving efforts and the circumstances under which they have emerged.
- *Experimental preservation activity* discusses significant practical experimentation in data archiving.
- *Preservation research* sets forth key areas for focused research and presents examples of projects in those areas.

### Common Understandings Among Stakeholders

Limited but highly influential agreements about key issues exist among those who take an interest in the long-term management of digital information—interests that are intrinsically, if at times confusingly, interrelated. Those who create or publish such information, those who wish to use the information, and those who act as archival repositories for it all have a stake in maintaining digital assets over time. They often have different purposes in mind when they speak of making the information accessible in the future, but they share the conviction that such longevity is highly desirable.

The interests of the creator or distributor, user, and repository are interrelated because each group has a formative influence over whether, how, and at what cost digital information will be made accessible over the long term. The first decisive factor is how digital information is created and distributed. This may determine whether, how, and at what cost the information can be preserved and made accessible to users over time. The choice of some formats may make it more difficult to manage the digital object and ensure future, or even current, access. The selection of simple or standard formats (e.g., PDF files, TIFF images, or ASCII text) can simplify certain storage issues.

Another deciding influence is how, to whom, and under what terms or conditions archived digital information is to be distributed.

This will determine how, by whom, and at what cost that information is created, distributed, and accessioned into an archive. Accordingly, preservation practice usually represents some ongoing negotiation between creators or publishers, archives, and users. Each stakeholder makes choices that can influence the long-term accessibility of a digital asset. The Inter-university Consortium for Political and Social Research (ICPSR), for example, was designed to ensure long-term access to important social science research data sets. This membership organization states that "to ensure that data resources are available to future generations of scholars, ICPSR preserves data, migrating them to new storage media as changes in technology warrant" (ICPSR, no date). To support its activity, ICPSR has a sustainable, mission-driven business model, and it defines criteria for data entry, use, and preservation within the framework of that model. It has worked successfully for 40 years.

Stakeholders have reached a common understanding about what constitutes a trusted digital repository and what activities the repository must routinely undertake, even though the way in which some of the basic preservation functions will be undertaken remains uncertain. A viable digital archival repository must have several attributes. For example, it must be explicit about what digital information it preserves, why, and for whom. It also must be clear about the attributes of the archived information it intends to preserve. It must offer services that meet the minimum requirements of data creators and users. It must be prepared to negotiate and accept deposits of appropriate digital information from those who create or distribute that information, and the terms of those negotiations must be clear to all. The repository must also obtain enough control of deposited information to ensure its long-term preservation; this responsibility may include gaining access to data in order to check on their integrity while protecting those same data from access by unauthorized parties. The repository must make information available to users under conditions negotiated and agreed on with depositors. Finally, given the rapidly changing technological environment in which the repository will take in and tend to digital information, it must seek new solutions as technology evolves.

Another area of common understanding is the emergence of the Open Archival Information System (OAIS) as the standard reference model. This model supplies a conceptual framework for discussing and describing archival practice. OAIS articulates the roles and interrelationships of the three groups that have a key stake in digital process, i.e., creator or distributor, user, and repository. The reference model identifies preservation as a process that begins when digital information is created; this is a critical point of difference from the standard analog model, which considers preservation much later in the life cycle of an artifact. Finally, the OAIS model identifies the core functions and organizational features of a digital archival repository. This has influenced perceptions of what constitutes a trusted archives. OAIS is on the International Organization for Standardization

(ISO) standards track and is the reference model of choice of those involved in digital preservation worldwide.

Today, there are four commonly understood technical approaches to digital preservation. These approaches are not mutually exclusive; indeed, there is an emerging consensus that all four approaches, and probably others not yet devised, will be deployed for the variety of digital object types and the demands for access to them.

*Migration.* In this approach, digital information is stored in software-independent formats. The information is reformatted as needed so that it can be accessed using current hardware and software. Most digital archival repositories rely almost wholly on data migration. It is doubtful that the strategy will work well for mixed media.

*Technology preservation.* Under this approach, data are preserved along with the hardware/software on which they depend. Given the variety of hardware and software platforms and the rate at which they change, this strategy generally is not believed to be economically viable. Still, many data rescue efforts (see Digital archaeology below) rely on the persistence of outmoded hardware and software.

*Emulation.* Often considered a form of technology preservation, emulation entails storing digital information alongside detailed information about how it looked, felt, and functioned in its original software/hardware environment. The look, feel, and functionality of the digital information are then "emulated" or re-created on successive generations of hardware/software. Emulation is particularly pertinent to mixed media. Individuals who are conducting research on the technical and economic viability of this approach include Jeff Rothenberg at the RAND Corporation and researchers at CAMiL-EON. Emulation is in the exploratory phase; it has never been successfully used for preservation in a sustainable way.

*Persistent object preservation.* The opposite of migration, persistent object preservation (POP) entails explicitly declaring the properties (e.g., content, structure, context, presentation) of the original digital information that ensure its persistence. Of the strategies listed here, POP is the only one that starts with and remains focused on preserving the digital information from its inception. Other strategies attempt to counter or overcome the generic technical problem of obsolescence.

Another important technical approach merits mention—digital archaeology or data mining. Although not a preservation strategy as such, digital archaeology enables digital information to be rescued or recovered from disks, tapes, and other storage media that are no longer readable as a result of physical deterioration, neglect, obsolescence, or similar reasons.

To remain viable over the long term, appropriate documentation or metadata must accompany digital information. Key preservation metadata initiatives are reviewed in a white paper by the Online Computer Library Center (OCLC) and the Research Libraries Group (RLG).[1]

---

[1] See http://www.rlg.org/longterm/index.html.

### Practical Preservation Activity

There are several practical preservation efforts underway that demonstrate the range of experience and expertise around the country.

Active preservation programs are under way in archives where preservation is often legally mandated. For example, the archives of national and state governments are legally bound to preserve selected records of government, including electronic records, in perpetuity. Business archives, such as those at financial, pharmaceutical, chemical, and other companies, may maintain records for legal and other reasons. Statutes of limitations often govern these mandates; consequently, such archives do not typically keep data in perpetuity as do government archives. These systems can be said to be more analogous to records management than to archiving; nonetheless, managing digital records even for seven years can provide technical challenges. Archives are also established at not-for-profit institutions, such as universities, that maintain records (including electronic records) for legal, business, and cultural reasons.[2]

Preservation is also under way in organizations in which data creators and producers perceive the long-term commercial value of digital information. Publishers such as Elsevier Science preserve the electronic scholarly journals they produce. The entertainment industry, most notably music and film companies, have large investments in digital assets that they wish to reuse over time, and they have developed digital asset management systems tailored for their specific needs.

Preservation programs also are active in organizations that perceive a noncommercial value of digital information for use and reuse. Libraries, archives, and museums that digitize objects in their collections for online presentation, for example, may seek to maintain those objects over time rather than to rescan them as they become obsolete.

In places where data archives and systems vendors see commercial possibilities in the provision, supply, and support of long-term data storage facilities, preservation has become vital to commercial development. Data warehousing is a cottage industry with numerous related trade associations, exhibitions, and certification procedures. Data archives are beginning to emerge in the library community; for example, both OCLC and RLG are considering offering data archiving facilities on a cost-recovery basis.

Specific research communities, where data creators are also data users and where both groups recognize the importance of being able to reuse research data, undertake large-scale preservation of their intellectual assets. Both the ICPSR and the Roper Center preserve social science and government statistical data.

There are also major preservation activities in communities where data creators and data users recognize their interdependence and the value of the digital information in which they maintain a

---

2 The National Archives and Records Administration's Center for Electronic Records is perhaps the largest government archive for electronic records (http://www.nara.gov/nara/electronic/).

common interest. Through PubMed Central, the National Library of Medicine acts as a digital archival repository for medical publications and other medical information.

Finally, archival repositories may be developed as a by-product of a commercial process. The Internet Archive is an archive of "snapshots" taken of selected Web pages by Alexa. An information company can use information gained from those snapshots for commercial purposes. Alexa assesses the visibility of Web pages by seeing who links into a site.

### *Experimental Preservation Activity*

The InterPARES (International Research on Permanent Authentic Records in Electronic Systems) Project is a major international research initiative involving archival scholars, computer engineering scholars, and representatives of national archival institutions and private industry. Its goal is "to develop the theoretical and methodological knowledge essential for the permanent preservation of records generated electronically, and, on the basis of this knowledge, to formulate model policies, strategies, and standards capable of ensuring their preservation." The InterPARES Project is investigating numerous issues in digital preservation, including the authenticity of electronic records.

The National Archives and Records Administration is developing a strategic and technical framework within which it may preserve in perpetuity selected electronic records of the federal government. It is closely involved with the InterPARES Project, the OAIS reference standard, the National Partnership for Advanced Computational Infrastructure led by the San Diego Super Computer Center, and others. It is an international leader in research in selected areas, including requirements and processes for the preservation and reproduction of authentic records, development of the persistent archives method, application of advanced computing tools to records-management processes, and integration of digital preservation technologies with infrastructure technologies for e-government and e-business.

Under the auspices of The Andrew W. Mellon Foundation's e-journal archiving program, seven major libraries (the New York Public Library and the university libraries of Cornell, Harvard, Massachusetts Institute of Technology [MIT], Pennsylvania, Stanford, and Yale) are engaged in planning digital archival repositories for different kinds of scholarly journals. Yale, Harvard, and Pennsylvania have worked with commercial publishers on archiving the full range of their electronic journals; Cornell and the New York Public Library have worked on archiving journals in specific disciplines. MIT's project involves archiving "dynamic" e-journals (i.e., those that change frequently), and Stanford is investigating the development of archiving software tools under the auspices of its LOCKSS (Lots of Copies Keep Stuff Safe) program.

RLG and OCLC are jointly conducting preservation research. At present, their work focuses on the attributes of a digital archival repository and on preservation metadata.

The Andrew W. Mellon Foundation has invested in an investigation of emulation as a viable preservation strategy. Jeff Rothenberg at the RAND Corporation is conducting this research.

The IBM Almaden Research Center is investigating the possibility of using a universal virtual machine for digital preservation.

The University of Pennsylvania is conducting work on data provenance.

### Preservation Research

There are currently nine areas of significant research into preserving digital files. They are:

1. Architecture and performance of archival repositories. Key research is under way at the San Diego Super Computer Center, Stanford University, the National Archives and Records Administration, the Culpeper Center of the Library of Congress, Cornell University, Yale University, MIT, and Harvard University.

2. Persistent identification of and naming for archived information (e.g., International Digital Object Identifier [DOI], Persistent Uniform Resource Locator [PURL]).

3. Methods for recording and ensuring authenticity of archived information (digital signatures, watermarking, mechanisms for recording information about provenance). Determining the authenticity of a digital object is likely to require the use of techniques whose reliability is still being debated. Techniques appropriate to digital images may include digital signatures and watermarking. Checksums and other technical routines that produce message digests are appropriate for objects in virtually all formats. They help determine authenticity by analyzing the object's structure and composition and whether it has been changed in any way since a particular benchmark point.

   Information may be found at

   • Authenticity in a Digital Environment (CLIR 2000). Report of a group of experts convened by CLIR to address the question: What is an authentic digital object? http://www.clir.org/pubs/reports/pub92/contents.html
   • The importance of verifying the authenticity of an information object is well described in The Evidence in Hand: Report of the Task Force on the Artifact in Library Collections (CLIR 2001) http://www.clir.org/activities/details/artifact-docs.html
   • MD5 unofficial home page http://userpages.umbc.edu/~mabzug1/cs/md5/md5.html
   • On checksum, see http://www.checksum.org/
   • On digital signatures, see http://www.w3.org/DSig/ and information from the Electronic Privacy Information Center
   • On digital watermarking, see The Information Hiding Homep-

age. Steganography and Digital Watermarking. Available at: http://www.cl.cam.ac.uk/~fapp2/steganography/.

4. Degradation and testing of magnetic and other media used to store digital information (work being conducted at the National Institute of Standards and Technology).

5. Attributes of preservable digital information. These efforts focus on specific kinds of digital information. For example, research communities interested in social science and in space data have defined standards for formatting and describing information in their respective fields.

6. Attributes of trusted digital archival repositories. This work centers on specific kinds of digital information and on the organizations that arise to preserve it. Participants in the Mellon e-journals archiving program, for example, are looking at the organizational, business, and rights issues that surround archives that are established to preserve scholarly e-journals.

7. Development of standards (including standards for data and metadata formats, digital storage media, and data management practice). Formal standardization takes place through bodies such as the ISO, World Wide Web Consortium (W3C), National Information Standards Organization (NISO), and Internet Engineering Task Force (IETF) and reflects the emerging consensus of stakeholder communities. It is important to distinguish between the standards themselves and the understandings that need to be reached among stakeholders about how the standards are to be applied in certain instances (see item 5).

8. Automatic copying and distribution of digital information (LOCKSS).

9. Policies and implementation mechanisms for the preservation risk management and assessment of Web-accessible content (Project Prism at Cornell University).

If preservation activity in the near future bears any resemblance to that activity in the past two years or so, there will be further significant and unpredictable changes in this dynamic field.

# References

ICPSR. No date. "About ICPSR." Available from http://www.icpsr.umich.edu/ORG/about.html.

*Web Sites Noted in Text*

Alexa. http://info.alexa.com

CAMiLEON. www.si.umich.edu/CAMILEON/

Cornell University. www.library.cornell.edu/preservation/
digital.html
http://rmc-www.library.cornell.edu/online/studentrecords/

Electronic Privacy Information Center. www.epic.org/

Elsevier e-journal archiving. www.elsevier.nl
www.elsevier.nl/homepage/about/resproj/tulip.shtml
www.diglib.org/preserve/yale0206.htm

Harvard University. www.news.harvard.edu/gazette/1999/03.25/
diglibrary.html

IBM Almaden Project: www.almaden.ibm.com

International Digital Object Identifier (DOI). www.doi.org

International Organization for Standardization (ISO). www.iso.org

Internet Archive. www.archive.org/about

Internet Engineering Task Force (IETF). www.ietf.org

InterPARES Project. www.interpares.org

Inter-university Consortium for Political and Social Research
(ICPSR). www.icpsr.umich.edu

Library of Congress National Audio-Visual Conservation Center in
Culpeper. http://lcweb.loc.gov/rr/mopic/avprot/avprhome.html

Lots of Copies Keep Stuff Safe (LOCKSS). http://lockss.stanford.edu

Massachusetts Institute of Technology (MIT). http://web.mit.edu/
newsoffice/nr/2000/libraries.html

Mellon e-journal archiving. www.diglib.org/preserve/ejp.htm

National Partnership for Advanced Computational Infrastructure
(NPACI). www.npaci.edu/online/v6.2/perm.html

National Archives and Records Administration (NARA).
www.nara.gov
www.nara.gov/nara/vision/eap/eapspec.html
www.nara.gov/nara/electronic

National Information Standards Organization (NISO). www.niso.org

National Institute of Standards and Technology (NIST).
www.nist.gov;
www.itl.nist.gov/div895

Online Computer Library Center (OCLC). www.oclc.org/research/
pmwg/

Open Archival Information System (OAIS) standard "reference model." http://ssdoo.gsfc.nasa.gov/nost/isoas/ref_model.html

Persistent Uniform Resource Locator (PURL). www.purl.org

Project Prism. http://prism.cornell.edu/PrismWeb/AboutPrism.htm

PubMed Central. www.pubmedcentral.nih.gov

Research Libraries Group (RLG). www.rlg.org/longterm/ndex.html;
www.rlg.org/pr/pr2000-oclc.html

Roper Center. www.ropercenter.uconn.edu/catalog40/
StartQuery.html

Rothenberg, Jeff (RAND Corporation). www.rand.org/
methodology/isg/archives.html

San Diego Super Computer Center. www.sdsc.edu/
DigitalLibraries.html

Stanford University. www.sul.stanford.edu/depts/spc/indaids.html

University of Pennsylvania (work on data provenance).
http://db.cis.upenn.edu/Research/provenance.html

World Wide Web Consortium (W3C). www.w3.org

Yale University. www.yale.edu/opa/newsr/01-02-23-02.all.html